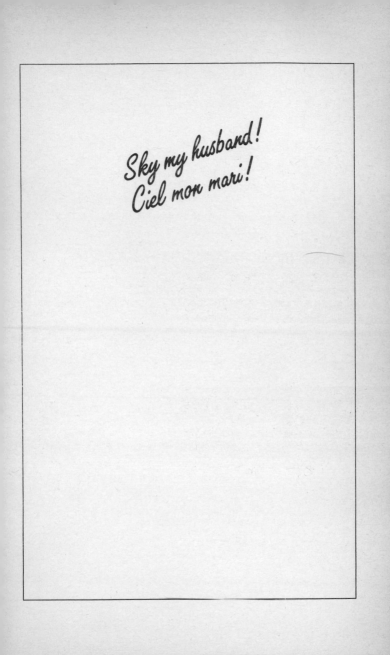

Sky my husband!
Ciel mon mari!

Du même auteur

La théière de Chardin
Garnier, 1979

L'allemaniaque de la France profonde
AMP Éditions, 1981

L'agenda du VIP
Garnier, 1982

La Khomenie du pouvoir
Scorpio, 1983

Sky my husband ! Ciel mon mari !
Hermé, 1985

Le guide du FDG
avec Marie Garagnoux
Hermé, 1986

Mon carnet secret FM
Carrère, 1986

Sky my teacher !
Carrère, 1987

JEAN-LOUP CHIFLET

Sky my husband!
Ciel mon mari!

GUIDE DE L'ANGLAIS COURANT

GUIDE OF THE RUNNING ENGLISH

DESSINS DE CLAB

Hermé

EN COUVERTURE : dessin de Clab
Photo Éditions Hermé

ISBN 2-02-009485-1
(ISBN 1re publication : 2-86665-020-4)

A Shakespeare,
Jane Birkin, Maurice Chevalier
et les autres...

PRÉFACE

Souvenez-vous, c'était la fin des années 50. La France, la vraie, la profonde, la « franchouillarde », celle du Piconbière et des congés payés à la « gueule d'atmosphère » se réveilla un beau matin de nouveau sous la botte ou plutôt, le chapeau melon de l'envahisseur : les FRANGLAIS avaient débarqué sur leurs yachts, envahissant notre douce France, détruisant tout sur leur passage à coups de bulldozers, violant à coups de sex-shops, embrochant la poule au pot à coups de barbecues, submergeant à coups de hot dogs les cafés du commerce qu'ils allèrent jusqu'à transformer en drugstores.

Monsieur Dupont-Durand était effondré. Il n'en croyait pas ses oreilles. Certes, il avait fini par s'habituer sans problème au chewing-gum des GI's libérateurs, ceux-là même qui dansaient le be-bop le week-end dans les dancings, mais là, ça devenait too much. Jamais la France n'avait été aussi humiliée par la perfide Albion depuis Jeanne d'Arc et Napoléon.

Heureusement, en 1964, la contre-attaque apparut sous la plume féroce d'Etiemble et son célèbre *Parlez-vous franglais ?*, terrible réquisitoire contre l'envahisseur. Il fut soutenu dans son courageux combat par l'inoubliable Fernand Reynaud et son *Restons français!* Grâce à ces farouches chevaliers, l'ennemi parut reculer mais en 1970 une nouvelle brèche apparut dans l'univers impitoyable du showbiz et du marketing où les meetings succédaient aux brainstormings, les box-offices aux hit-parades.

C'en était trop! Le gouvernement français prit lui-même les choses en main, faisant voter une loi qui, en 1977, interdit l'usage des mots anglais dans le vocabulaire officiel, transformant pêle-mêle bulldozer en *bouteur*, marketing en *mercatique*, l'interview du speaker en *entretien de l'annonceur* et le container en *conteneur*.

Mais c'était trop tard! La « franglisation » avait atteint son point de non-retour et personne ne pouvait plus empêcher monsieur Dupont-Durand de faire son jogging autour du parking. Même monsieur Robert, celui du dictionnaire, continuait de définir tranquillement dans son vénérable ouvrage une personne « sexy » comme « ayant du sex-appeal ». C'était un comble!

Mais était-ce donc si grave ? Ne valait-il pas mieux en rire ? Après tout, notre vaillant pays en avait vu d'autres et, comme chacun sait en France, si on n'a pas de pétrole et encore moins de vocabulaire, on a des idées et encore plus d'humour. Puisque l'anglais était là, on allait le cuisiner à la française et se le mitonner suivant une recette dont je vous livre le secret :

« Prendre un mot français, normal, au sens propre ou au sens figuré suivant la saison et les arrivages.
Chercher sa traduction littérale. Si l'on en trouve plusieurs, faire un choix arbitraire.
Introduire ce mot dans une locution courante (proverbe, expression officielle ou familière, citation, etc.). Si l'on aime les plats relevés, ne pas hésiter à parsemer d'argot.
Traduire la locution entière mot à mot.
Servir. »

Voilà, j'ai passé ces dernières années à élaborer et à tester patiemment, dans l'ombre de mon laboratoire, des recettes de cette nouvelle gastronomie. Celle qui me paraît la plus succulente a donné son titre à ce livre...
Quant aux autres, je vous laisse juge...

A la bonne vôtre ! (At the good yours !)

Jean-Loup Chiflet   John-Wolf Whistle

AVERTISSEMENT *WARNING*

Cher lecteur,

Avant de vous plonger à corps perdu (at lost body) dans ce fabuleux guide de l'anglais courant, apprenez à vous en servir et à en tirer un maximum pour être très vite à tu et à toi (to you and to you) avec vos interlocuteurs anglophones.

Ce guide se lit de gauche à droite et de A à Z.

Vous trouverez ci-contre un schéma explicite qui devrait vous éclairer définitivement sur son utilisation.

Cet ouvrage étant également une méthode d'apprentissage de la langue, vous aurez la possibilité de vérifier les progrès de vos connaissances grâce aux exercices récapitulatifs qui jalonnent l'ouvrage.

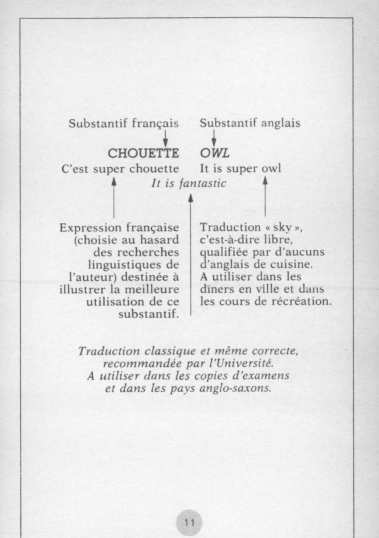

Substantif français   Substantif anglais

CHOUETTE   *OWL*

C'est super chouette   It is super owl

It is fantastic

Expression française (choisie au hasard des recherches linguistiques de l'auteur) destinée à illustrer la meilleure utilisation de ce substantif.

Traduction « sky », c'est-à-dire libre, qualifiée par d'aucuns d'anglais de cuisine. A utiliser dans les dîners en ville et dans les cours de récréation.

Traduction classique et même correcte, recommandée par l'Université. A utiliser dans les copies d'examens et dans les pays anglo-saxons.

Première leçon
A

ABOIS   *BARKS*
Être aux abois   To be at the barks
To be at your last gasp

AFFICHE   *POSTER*
Tenir l'affiche   To hold the poster
To have a long run

ALLER   *TO GO*
Ça ira, ça ira !   It will go, it will go
French revolutionary slogan

ÂNE   *DONKEY*

Passer du coq à l'âne   To pass from cock to donkey

To change the subject

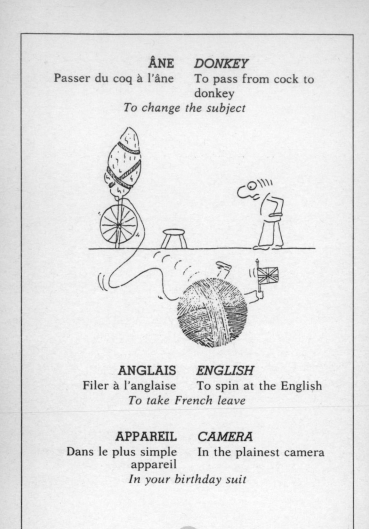

ANGLAIS   *ENGLISH*

Filer à l'anglaise   To spin at the English

To take French leave

APPAREIL   *CAMERA*

Dans le plus simple appareil   In the plainest camera

In your birthday suit

ARRACHER *TO PULL OUT*

Travailler d'arrache-pied To work of pull out foot

To work like a navvy

ASSIETTE *PLATE*

Ne pas être dans son assiette Not to be in one's plate

To be out of sorts

AUBERGE *INN*

Nous ne sommes pas sortis de l'auberge We are not out of the inn

We are not out of the wood

15

Deuxième leçon
B

BAC *FERRY*
Passer son bac To pass one's ferry
To graduate

BAIN *BATH*
Au bain-marie At the bath-Mary
A water bath

BALADER *TO GO FOR A WALK*
Il a les mains baladeuses He has the hands going
for a walk
He has wandering palms

BALAI *BROOM*
Il a cinquante balais He has fifty brooms
He is fifty

16

BALANCE *SCALES*
Je m'en contre-balance — I am counter-scaling
I don't give a damn

BALANCER *TO SWING*
Balancer une vanne — To swing a sluice
To make a dig

Être bien balancée — To be well swung
To be well built

BALEINE *WHALE*
Une baleine de parapluie — A whale of umbrella
An umbrella spoke

BANDE *GANG*
Une bande Velpeau — A Velpeau gang
A bandage

BARBE *BEARD*
Etre barbant — To be bearding
To be boring

La barbe! — The beard!
What a bore!

Au nez et à la barbe de quelqu'un — At the nose and at the beard of somebody
To be under your nose

BATEAU   *BOAT*

Il m'a monté un bateau   He went me up a boat
He led me up the garden path

BÂTIMENT   *BUILDING*

Quand le bâtiment va, tout va !   When the building goes, everything goes !
French idiom which means that the economy is going well

BAVER   *TO SLAVER*

En baver des ronds de chapeau   To slaver rounds of hat
To have your tongue hanging out

BEC   *BEAK*

Tomber sur un bec   To fall on a beak
To come up against a snag
Clouer le bec   To nail the beak
To shut someone up

BÊCHER   *TO DIG*

Un bêcheur   A digger
Toffee nosed

BERGÈRE   *SHEPHERDESS*

Les Folies Bergère   The Shepherdess Madnesses
Very famous French cabaret

BESOIN *NEED*
Faire ses besoins To do one's needs
To spend a penny

BÊTE *BEAST*
Chercher la petite bête To look for the little
beast
To nit-pick

BEURRE *BUTTER*
Etre beurré To be buttered
To be pickled

BIDE (familier) *STOMACH*
Faire un bide To make a stomach
To have egg on your face

BIDON *JERRICAN*
C'est bidon It is jerrican
It's baloney

Se bidonner To jerrican one's self
To laugh

BLANC *WHITE*
Faire chou blanc To make white cabbage
To fail completely

BLEU *BLUE*

N'y voir que du bleu   To see only blue
Not to smell a rat

BŒUF *BEEF*

Un effet bœuf   A beef effect
An impressive effect

BOMBE *BOMB*

Aller faire la bombe   To go and make the bomb
To paint the town red

BON *GOOD*

Y'a bon Banania!   There is good Banania!
Famous advertising slogan

BOND *JUMP*

Faire faux bond   To make wrong jump
To stand someone up

BONHOMME   *GENTLEMAN*

Aller son petit
bonhomme de chemin

To go one's little
gentleman of path

To tootle along

BOUCHER   *TO CORK*

En boucher un coin   To cork a corner

To knock someone sideways

BOUQUET   *BUNCH*

C'est le bouquet !   It is the bunch !

That takes the biscuit !

BOURSE   *STOCK EXCHANGE*

La bourse ou la vie !

The stock exchange
or the life !

Your money or your life !

BOUTEILLE   *BOTTLE*

Avoir de la bouteille   To have some bottle

To be long in the tooth

BRAS   *ARM*

A bras-le-corps   At arm, the body

Arms round the waist

BUT   *GOAL*

De but en blanc   From goal to white

At the drop of a hat

He span at the English in the plainest camera at our nose and our beard because he was buttered and we were looking for the little beast in swinging him a sluice.

Il a filé à l'anglaise dans le plus simple appareil à notre nez et à notre barbe parce qu'il était beurré et nous cherchions la petite bête en lui balançant une vanne.

Troisième leçon
C

ÇA — *THAT*
Je ne pense qu'à ça — I only think of that
I have a dirty mind

CACHET — *PILL*
Le cachet de la poste faisant foi — The pill of the mail making faith
Date as post mark

CADAVRE — *CORPSE*
Un cadavre ambulant — A travelling corpse
Death warmed up

CAFARD — *COCKROACH*
Avoir le cafard — To have the cockroach
To have the blues

CAISSE   *CASH*

Jouer de la grosse caisse   To play big cash

To play bass-drum

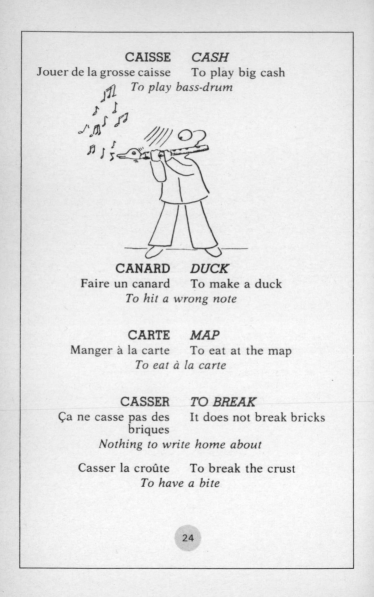

CANARD   *DUCK*

Faire un canard   To make a duck

To hit a wrong note

CARTE   *MAP*

Manger à la carte   To eat at the map

To eat à la carte

CASSER   *TO BREAK*

Ça ne casse pas des briques   It does not break bricks

Nothing to write home about

Casser la croûte   To break the crust

To have a bite

CATHOLIQUE *CATHOLIC*
Ne pas avoir l'air   To look Anglican
catholique
To look shady

CAUSER *TO SPEAK*
Causes toujours,   Speak always, you are
tu m'intéresses   interesting me
You can always talk, you don't impress me

CHAGRIN *SORROW*
Une peau de chagrin   A skin of sorrow
Shagreen

CHAMPIGNON *MUSHROOM*
Appuyer sur le   To press on the
champignon   mushroom
To accelerate

CHASSE *HUNT*
Tirer la chasse   To pull the hunt
To flush

CHEF *CHIEF*
Au premier chef At the first chief
Essentially

CHEVAL *HORSE*
Ce n'est pas le mauvais He is not the bad horse
cheval
He is not a bad guy

CHEVILLE *ANKLE*
La cheville ouvrière The worker ankle
The king pin

CHÈVRE *GOAT*
Chèvrefeuille Goatleaf
Honeysuckle

CHIEN *DOG*
Avoir du chien To have dog
To be sexy

CHOCOLAT — *CHOCOLATE*

Etre chocolat — To be chocolate
To have been swindled

CHOSE — *THING*

Je me sens tout chose — I feel all thing
I feel under the weather

CHOU — *CABBAGE*

C'est son chou-chou — He is her cabbage-cabbage
He is her pet

Chou à la crème — Cabbage at the cream
Cream puff

CHOUETTE — *OWL*

C'est super chouette — It is super owl
It is fantastic

CIRCULATION — *TRAFFIC*

Avoir une mauvaise circulation — To have a bad traffic
To have bad blood circulation

CIRER — *TO POLISH*

Rien à cirer — Nothing to polish
Not to give a damn

CLIQUES   *CLICKS*

Prendre ses cliques et ses claques   To take one's clicks and one's clacks

To clean up and clear out

CLOCHE   *BELL*

Déménager à la cloche de bois   To move at the wooden bell

To do a moonlight flit

COCHON   *PIG*

Copains comme cochons   Friends like pigs

Inseparable friends

COIN   *CORNER*

Aller au petit coin   To go to the little corner

To go to the loo

Coin-coin   Corner-corner

Quack

COMMISSION   *COMMISSION*

Faire les commissions   To make commissions

To go shopping

COMMODE   *CHEST OF DRAWERS*

Ce n'est pas commode   It is not chest of drawers

It is not easy

COMPTER   *TO COUNT*

Compter pour du beurre   To count for butter
To count for nothing

Son compte est bon   His count is good
He has had it

CONCERT   *CONCERT*

Aller de concert   To go of concert
To go together

CONSEIL   *ADVICE*

Un conseil d'administration   An advice of administration
A board of directors

CONTRAVENTION   *TICKET*

Faire sauter une contravention   To make a ticket jump
Using influence to avoid penalty

COUCHE (littéraire)   *BED*
Il en tient une couche   He is holding a bed
He is a cretin

COURANT   *CURRENT*
Tenez-moi au courant   Keep me at the current
Keep me informed

COURIR   *TO RUN*
Courir sur le haricot   To run on the bean
To get on someone's nerves

CRÊPE   *PANCAKE*
Crêper le chignon   To pancake the bun
To fight (among women)

CROIX   *CROSS*
Croix de bois,   Wooden cross,
croix de fer,   iron cross,
si je mens je vais en enfer   if I lie I go to hell
Cross my heart and hope to die

CUIRE   *TO COOK*
C'est du tout cuit   It is all cooked
It's in the bag

Être dur à cuire   To be hard to cook
To put up a strong resistance

Les carottes sont cuites   The carrots are cooked
The die is cast

CUL   *ASS*

Cul de sac   Ass of bag
Cul de sac

Bouche en cul de poule   Mouth in ass of chicken
Pursed lips

Faire cul sec   To do dry ass
To down in one

Etre comme cul et   To be like ass and shirt
chemise
To be best friends

Tirer au cul   To pull at the ass
To swing the lead

La digue du cul   The pier of the ass
Words of a famous French popular song

La peau du cul   The skin of the ass
Very expensive

31

Révision
B-C

Because he was only thinking of that, he
took his clicks and his clacks to move at
the wooden bell to a super owl girl who
had dog. He became her cabbage-cabbage
and they are now like ass and shirt.

Parce qu'il ne pensait qu'à ça, il prit ses
cliques et ses claques pour déménager à
la cloche de bois pour une super fille
chouette qui avait du chien. Il devint son
chou-chou et ils sont maintenant comme
cul et chemise.

Quatrième leçon
D

DÉFAUT   *DEFECT*
Faire défaut   To do defect
To lack

DEMAIN   *TOMORROW*
Ce n'est pas demain la   It is not tomorrow the
veille   day before
Not to be about to do something

DEMEURE   *MANSION*
Mettre en demeure   To put in mansion
To oblige

DENT   *TOOTH*
Avoir une dent contre   To have a tooth
quelqu'un   opposite somebody
To have something against somebody

DEVANT   *IN FRONT*
Gros Jean comme devant   Big John like in front
Like a booby

DIEU   *GOD*
Vingt dieux,   Twenty gods,
la belle église !   the nice church !
Wow, what a scorcher!

DIRE   *TO SAY*
Le qu'en-dira-t-on   The what-will-one-say
What will the neighbours say

DRAP   *BED SHEET*
Etre dans de beaux draps   To be in nice bed sheets
To be in a fix

Cinquième leçon
E

EMPRUNTER   *TO BORROW*
Avoir un air emprunté   To have a borrowed air
To look uncomfortable

Emprunter une route   To borrow a road
To take a road

ENREGISTRER   *TO RECORD*
Enregistrer ses bagages   To record one's luggage
To check in baggage

ENTENDRE   *TO HEAR*
A bon entendeur, salut !   At good hearer, goodbye !
Once and for all, goodbye!

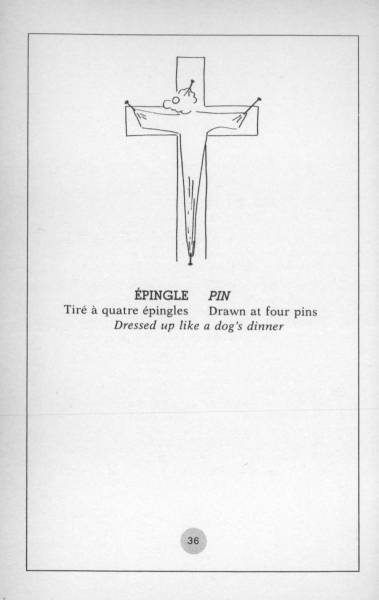

ÉPINGLE   *PIN*
Tiré à quatre épingles   Drawn at four pins
Dressed up like a dog's dinner

Sixième leçon
F

FACTURE   *INVOICE*
Etre de bonne facture   To be of good invoice
To be of good quality

FAIRE   *TO MAKE*
Fait comme un rat   Made like a rat
To be cornered

Faire le beau   To make the nice
To beg

FER   *IRON*
Un chemin de fer   A path of iron
A railway

FESSE   *BUTTOCK*
Un fesse-Mathieu   A buttock-Matthew
A skinflint

FEUILLE   *LEAF*
Dur de la feuille   Hard of the leaf
Hard of hearing

FIER   *PROUD*
Fier-à-bras   Proud-to-arm
A wise guy

FIL   *THREAD*
Aller au fil de l'eau   To go at the thread of
water
To drift

Passer au fil de l'épée   To pass at the thread
of the sword
To run someone through with a sword

Un coup de fil   A knock of thread
A phone call

FILET   *NET*
Un faux-filet   A wrong net
A type of steak

FINIR   *TO FINISH*
Finir en beauté   To finish in beauty
To end in glory

FLEUR   *FLOWER*
Elle est « fleur bleue »   She is « blue flower »
A prude

Un chou-fleur   A cabbage-flower
A cauliflower

FOIE   *LIVER*
Avoir les foies   To have the livers
To be scared stiff

FOND   *BOTTOM*
Aller à fond de train   To go at bottom of train
To go flat out

FOUR   *OVEN*
Un petit four   A little oven
A small cake

FRAIS   *COOL*
Aux frais de la Princesse   At the cool of the
Princess
At Her Majesty's expense

Faire les frais de la   To do the cool of the
conversation   conversation
To lead the conversation

Les frais généraux   The general cool
The overheads

FRAISE   *STRAWBERRY*
Sucrer les fraises   To sugar the
strawberries
To be old and doddery

Ramener sa fraise   To bring back one's
strawberry
To show up

FRANC   *FRANK*
Pas franc du collier   Not frank of the collar
Fishy

FRANCHISE   *FRANKNESS*
La franchise postale   The mailed frankness
Freepost

FROID *COLD*
Un froid de canard   A cold of duck
Brass monkey weather

Septième leçon
G

GAFFE   *HOOK*
Faire une gaffe   To do a hook
To make a blunder

GAGNER   *TO WIN*
Un gagne-pain   A win-bread
A job which pays the bills

GARDER   *TO KEEP*
Garde-à-vous !   Keep to you !
Attention !

Garder un chien de sa chienne   To keep a dog from one's bitch
To have it in for someone

GARE *STATION*

Sans crier gare Without shouting station
Without warning

GAUCHE *LEFT*

Passer l'arme à gauche To pass the weapon to
the left
To kick the bucket

GONFLER *TO INFLATE*

Il est vachement gonflé He is cowly inflated
He has got a cheek

GORGE *THROAT*

Faire des gorges chaudes To do warm throats
To keep people talking

GROS *BIG*

Acheter en gros To buy in big
To buy wholesale

GUÉ *FORD*

La bonne aventure au The good adventure at
gué! the ford!
Traditional French folk song

GUÊPE *WASP*

Pas folle la guêpe! Not crazy the wasp!
Not born yesterday

GUERRE *WAR*

De guerre lasse From tired war
Finally

C'est de bonne guerre It is of good war
Fair's fair

Révision
D à G

He has the livers because he is made like a rat. He has been put in mansion to give back the little oven, the wrong net and the cabbage-flower stolen in the market.

Il a les foies parce qu'il est fait comme un rat. Il a été mis en demeure de rendre le petit four, le faux-filet et le chou-fleur volés au marché.

Huitième leçon
H-I

HALEINE   *BREATH*
De longue haleine   Of long breath
Long term

HANNETON   *BEETLE*
Pas piqué des   Not picked of the
    hannetons !   beetles !
A helluva...

HARICOTS   *BEANS*
La fin des haricots   The end of the beans
The last straw

HAUT   *HIGH*
Tenir le haut du pavé   To hold the high of the
    pavement
To lord it

HEURE   *HOUR*
A la bonne heure !   At the good hour !
Well done!

HUILE   *OIL*
Ça baigne dans l'huile   It is bathing in the oil
Everything is going smoothly

INCENDIER   *TO BURN DOWN*
Je me suis fait incendier   I have been burnt down
I have been caught

Neuvième leçon
J-K

JAMBE   *LEG*

Ça me fait une belle jambe   It makes me a nice leg

It won't get me very far

Faire des ronds de jambes   To make rounds of legs

To bow and scrape

JAUNE   *YELLOW*

Rire jaune   To laugh yellow

To give a forced laugh

JEU   *GAME*

Le jeu n'en vaut pas la chandelle   The game is not worth the candle

It is not worth it

Etre vieux jeu   To be old game

To be old-fashioned

JONC *RUSH*

Tu me pèles le jonc ! You are peeling my
rush !

You get up my nose !

JOUER *TO PLAY*

Jouer son va-tout To play one's go all

To play one's last card

KIF *MARIJUANA*

Kif-kif bourricot Marijuana-marijuana
donkey

It is the same thing

Dixième leçon
L

LÀ   *HERE*

Une Marie-couche-toi-là   A Mary-sleep-here

A tart

LAMPE   *LAMP*

S'en mettre plein la lampe   To fill plenty one's lamp

To stuff one's face

LANGUE   *TONGUE*

Langue vivante   Living tongue
A spoken language

Avoir une langue bien pendue   To have a well hanged tongue
A chatter box

Prendre langue   To take tongue
To speak to

LARGE   *WIDE*

Ne pas en mener large   Not to lead wide
To be scared

LÉGUME   *VEGETABLE*

Une grosse légume   A big vegetable
A V.I.P.

LETTRE   *LETTER*

Au pied de la lettre   At the foot of the letter
Literally

Avoir des lettres   To have letters
A cultivated person

LIEU   *PLACE*

J'ai tout lieu de croire   I have all place to believe
Everything leads me to believe

LIÈVRE *HARE*

Soulever un lièvre To lift up a hare
To stir up a hornet's nest

LIGNE *LINE*

Entrer en ligne de To enter in line of count
compte
To enter into consideration

LOURD *HEAVY*

Ne pas en savoir lourd Not to know heavy
about
Not to know much about

Révision
H à L

I have all place to believe that he is a big vegetable who has a well hanged tongue and who holds the high of the pavement in filling plenty his lamp.

J'ai tout lieu de croire que c'est une grosse légume qui a une langue bien pendue et qui tient le haut du pavé en s'en mettant plein la lampe.

Onzième leçon
M

MÂCHER *TO CHEW*
Ne pas mâcher ses mots Not to chew one's words
No to mince words

MAILLE *STITCH*
Avoir maille à partir To have stitch to leave
To have a bone to pick with

MANGER *TO EAT*
(familier : bouffer)
Cullottes bouffantes Eating pants
Baggy pants

MAIN   *HAND*

Haut la main   High the hand
Easily

Une petite main   A small hand
A dressmaker's apprentice

Passer la main dans le dos   To pass the hand in the back
To flatter

MAISON   *HOUSE*

C'est gros comme une maison   It is big like a house
It is as plain as the nose on your face

MAÎTRE   *MASTER*

Pour un coup d'essai, c'est un coup de maître   For a blow of try, it is a blow of master
It is a very good first attempt

MAL   *BAD*

Avoir le mal du pays   To have the bad of the country
To be homesick

Etre mal en point   To be bad in point
To be poorly

Faire mal à quelqu'un   To do bad to somebody
To hurt someone

MALHEUR   *BAD LUCK*

Faire un malheur   To do a bad luck
To be very successful

MANCHE   *SLEEVE*

Ne jetez pas le manche   Don't throw the sleeve
après la cognée   after the axe
Don't put the cart before the horse

La première manche   The first sleeve
The first set

MANDAT   *MONEY-ORDER*

Un mandat d'amener   A money-order to bring
Writ of arrest

MARCHE   *STEP*

Mettre en marche   To put in step
To start up

MARCHER   *TO WALK*

Faire marcher à la   To make walk at the
baguette   stick
To rule someone with a rod of iron

MARI   *HUSBAND*

Ciel mon mari!   Sky my husband!
My god! My husband!

MARRON   *BROWN*

Un avocat marron   A brown avocado
A shady lawyer

MARTEAU   *HAMMER*

Etre marteau   To be hammer
To be crazy

MEILLEUR   *BEST*

J'en passe,   I am passing some,
et des meilleures!   and of the best!
And that's not all!

MÊME   *SAME*

Etre à même   To be at the same
To be able to

C'est du pareil au   It is the same to the
même   same
To be as broad as it is long

MER *SEA*

Ce n'est pas la mer à boire · It is not the sea to drink

It is not that difficult

METTRE *TO PUT*

Sauver la mise · To save the put

To get back one's outlay

MONDE *WORLD*

Il y a du monde au balcon · There is some world at the balcony

Big busted

MONSIEUR *GENTLEMAN*

Un croque-monsieur · A bite-gentleman

A toasted ham and cheese sandwich

MONTER *TO GO UP*

Monter en épingle · To go up in pin

To make a mountain out of a molehill

MORT — *DEATH*

A l'article de la mort — At the article of the death
At the point of death

MOT — *WORD*

Toucher un mot — To touch a word
To mention

Ne pas dire un traître mot — Not to say a traitor word
Not to say a single word

MOUCHE — *FLY*

Prendre la mouche — To take the fly
To get huffy

Faire mouche — To do fly
To hit the bull's eye

Etre une fine mouche — To be a fine fly
Sly minx

MOURIR — *TO DIE*

Mourir à petit feu — To die at little fire
To fade away

MUR — *WALL*

Raser les murs — To shave the walls
To be hangdog

Douzième leçon
N

NEZ   *NOSE*

Faire un pied de nez   To make a foot of nose
To thumb your nose

NŒUD   *KNOT*

A la mords-moi le nœud   At the bite me the knot
Dodgy

Un sac de nœuds   A bag of knots
A problem

NOIR   *BLACK*

Broyer du noir   To crush black
To be depressed

NOM   *NAME*

Un nom à coucher dehors   A name to sleep outside
An impossible name

Révision
M-N

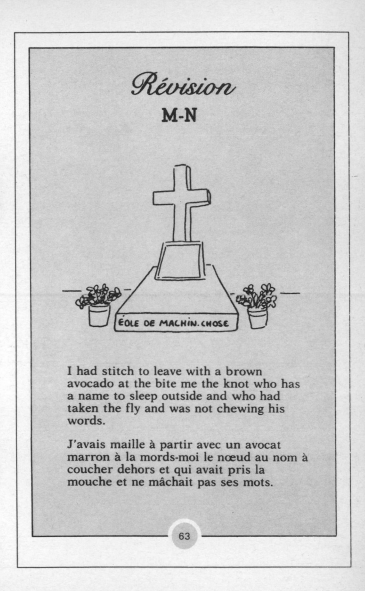

I had stitch to leave with a brown
avocado at the bite me the knot who has
a name to sleep outside and who had
taken the fly and was not chewing his
words.

J'avais maille à partir avec un avocat
marron à la mords-moi le nœud au nom à
coucher dehors et qui avait pris la
mouche et ne mâchait pas ses mots.

Treizième leçon

O

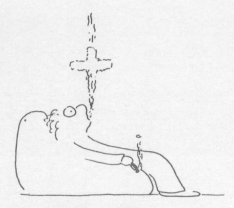

ODEUR   *SMELL*
En odeur de sainteté   In smell of holiness
In somebody's good graces

ŒIL   *EYE*
Avoir le coup d'œil   To have the blow of eye
To have a good eye

Œil de bœuf   Eye of beef
A round dormer window

Je m'en bats l'œil   I beat my eye
I don't care a hoot

Coûter les yeux de la tête   To cost the eyes of the head
To be very expensive

ŒUVRE   *WORK*
Un chef-d'œuvre   A chief of work
A masterpiece

OREILLE   *EAR*
Avoir la puce à l'oreille   To have the flea at the ear
To suspect

ORIGINE   *ORIGIN*
Rejoindre son corps d'origine   To rejoin one's origin's body
To rejoin one's regiment

OS   *BONE*
Tomber sur un os   To fall down on a bone
To hit a problem

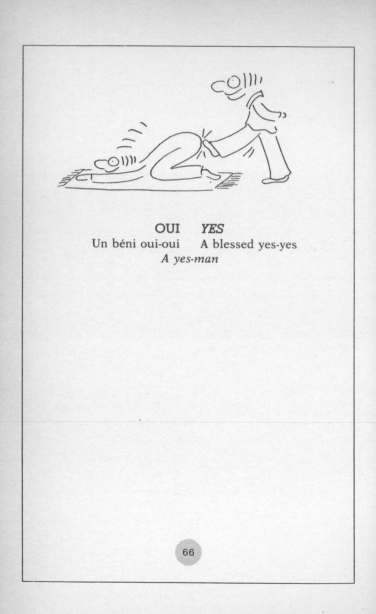

OUI   *YES*
Un béni oui-oui   A blessed yes-yes
A yes-man

PAIN   *BREAD*

Ça ne mange pas de pain   It doesn't eat bread

It is not important

PAPIER   *PAPER*

Etre dans les petits   To be in the little
papiers de quelqu'un   papers of somebody

To be in somebody's good books

PAQUET — *PACKAGE*

Mettre le paquet — To put the package
To pull out all the stops

PARFUM — *PERFUME*

Etre au parfum — To be at the perfume
To be aware of

PARLER — *TO SPEAK*

Parler à bâtons rompus — To speak at broken sticks
To speak a lot

Tu parles Charles ! — You speak Charles !
You don't say!

PASSER — *TO PASS*

Passer sur le billard — To pass on the billard
To have an operation

Passer à la casserole — To pass in the pan
To be killed or to get laid

Maison de passe — House of pass
Disorderly house

PÊCHE — *PEACH*

Je n'ai pas la pêche — I do not have the peach
I am a bit down

PÉDALER   *TO PEDAL*

Pédaler dans la choucroute   To pedal in the sauerkraut

To be mixed up

PEINTURE   *PAINTING*

Ne pas pouvoir voir quelqu'un en peinture   Not be able to see somebody in painting

To hate somebody

PELLICULE   *FILM*

Avoir des pellicules   To have films

To have dandruff

PENSER   *TO THINK*

Un pense-bête   A think-silly

A reminder

PERDRE   *TO LOSE*
Perdre la boule   To lose the bowl
To go crazy

PÈRE   *FATHER*
Allez donc, ce n'est pas   Go then, he is not my
mon père !   father !
I don't care !

PETIT   *LITTLE*
Au petit bonheur,   At the little luck,
la chance   the chance
At random

PIÈCE   *COIN*
Pièce rapportée   Brought-back coin
Relation by marriage

PIED   *FOOT*

A cloche-pied   At bell-foot
To hop

De pied en cap   From foot to cape
Elegant

Un casse-pieds   A break-feet
A bore

Prendre son pied   To take one's foot
To have it away

PILE   *BATTERY*

Tomber pile   To fall battery
To happen at the right moment

PIPE   *PIPE*

Nom d'une pipe!   Name of a pipe!
My god!

PLAISIR *PLEASURE*

Au plaisir,   At the pleasure,
ces messieurs-dames!   these gentlemen-ladies!
See you later!

PLANCHE *BOARD*

Plancher   To board
To be called up to the blackboard

Une planche pourrie   A rotten board
A dubious character

PLANTER *TO PLANT*

Se planter   To plant oneself
To fail

PLAT *DISH*

Tomber à plat   To fall at dish
To fall unluckily

Etre à plat   To be dished
To be washed out

Faire du plat à quelqu'un   To make dish to
somebody
To chat up

PLAT *FLAT*

Battre à plate couture   To beat at flat seam
To beat someone hollow

72

PLEIN   *FULL*

En mettre plein la vue   To put full of sight
To dazzle someone

PLIER   *TO FOLD*

Plier bagage   To fold luggage
To leave

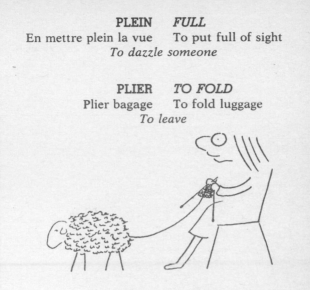

POIL   *HAIR*

Etre à poil   To be at hair
To be naked

Reprendre du poil de la bête   To take back the hair from the beast
To be one's own self again

POIREAU   *LEEK*

Faire le poireau   To make the leek
To wait for someone

POMPE *PUMP*

Aller à toute pompe   To go at all pump
To go very fast

Etre en dehors de ses   To be out of one's
pompes   pumps
To be absent minded

PORTRAIT *PICTURE*

Un portrait tout craché   A picture all spat
The spitting image

POSER *TO PUT DOWN*

Poser un lapin   To put down a rabbit
To stand someone up

POSTE *MAIL*

Rejoindre son poste   To go back to one's
mail
To rejoin one's regiment

Un bon poste   A good mail
A good job

POT   *POT*
Un pot-au-feu   A pot at the fire
Hot pot

Pot de vin   Pot of wine
A backhander

A la fortune du pot   At the fortune of the pot
To take potluck

Avoir du pot   To have pot
To be lucky

POUCE   *THUMB*
Pouce !   Thumb !
Pax !

POULE   *CHICKEN*
Pied-de-poule   Foot of chicken
Dog tooth check

Une poule mouillée   A wet chicken
A coward

Poule de luxe   Luxurious chicken
A high class call girl

Chair de poule   Flesh of chicken
Goose flesh

POUSSER   *TO PUSH*

A la va-comme-je-te-pousse   At the go like I push you

Any which way

PRISE   *PLUG*

Une prise de bec   A plug of beak

An argument

Etre aux prises   To be at the plugs

To be at grips with

PROCHAIN   *NEXT*

Aimer son prochain   To love one's next

To love one's neighbour

PROPRE   *CLEAN*

C'est du propre !   It is clean !

Well done ! (ironical)

Un propre à rien   A clean to nothing

A no-good

Quinzième leçon
Q

QUART   *QUARTER*

Au quart de tour   At the quarter of turn
Immediately

QUATORZE   *FOURTEEN*

C'est parti comme en   It is gone like in
quatorze   fourteen
It's started well

QUATRE   *FOUR*

Se mettre en quatre   To put oneself in four
To bend over backwards

QUELQU'UN   *SOMEBODY*

Avoir quelqu'un à la   To have somebody at
bonne   the good
To be fond of somebody

I don't have the peach because I am going to pass on the billiard. I have the flesh of chicken because it will cost me the eyes of the head and I will be obliged after to walk at bell-foot.

Je n'ai pas la pêche car je vais passer sur le billard. J'ai la chair de poule car cela me coûtera les yeux de la tête et après je serai obligé de marcher à cloche-pied.

Seizième leçon
R

RAISIN   *GRAPE*

Mi-figue, mi-raisin   Half-fig, half-grape

Neither fish nor fowl

RAPPORT   *REPORT*

Avoir des rapports sexuels   To have sexual reports

To have sexual relations

RAT   *RAT*

Etre fait comme un rat   To be made like a rat
To be done for

A bon chat, bon rat   At good cat, good rat
I have got your number

Donner sa langue au chat   To give one's tongue to
the cat
To give up

RAYER   *TO SCRATCH*

Un complet rayé   A scratched complete
A pin striped suit

Rayé des cadres   Scratched from the
frames
Struck off the list

RAYON   *X RAY*

En connaître un rayon   To know one X ray
To know a lot

RECETTE *RECIPE*
Faire recette To make recipe
To take money (for a theater)

REGARD *LOOK*
Couler un regard To flow a look
To cast a glance

REGARDER *TO LOOK*
Il n'est pas regardant He is not looking
He is not fussy

RÉGIME *DIET*
Un régime de bananes A bananas diet
A bunch of bananas

REIN *KIDNEY*
Un tour de reins A turn of kidneys
A sudden back pain

RENVOYER *TO SEND BACK*
Faire un renvoi To make a sent back
To belch

RÉSERVER *TO BOOK*
Etre réservé To be booked
To be shy

REVENIR   *TO COME BACK*
Un prix de revient   A price of come back
Cost price

RHUME   *COLD*
Un rhume carabiné   A rifled cold
A bad cold

ROMAINE   *ROMAN*
Bon comme la romaine   Good like the roman
Done for

ROND   *ROUND*
Rond comme une   Round like a tail of
queue de pelle   shovel
Very drunk

RONGER   *TO GNAW*
Ronger son frein   To gnaw one's brake
To champ at the bit

ROUE *WHEEL*

Sur les chapeaux de roue   On the hats of wheels
Very fast

RUE *STREET*

Ça ne court pas les rues   It doesn't run the streets
To be rare

Dix-septième leçon
S

SAC   *BAG*
Mettre à sac   To put to bag
To rifle

SALUT   *HELLO*
Une planche de salut   A board of hello
A life line

SAVON   *SOAP*
Passer un savon   To pass a soap
To shout at

SECOUER   *TO SHAKE*
Rien à secouer   Nothing to shake
It is not my problem

SENS   *WAY*
Avoir du bon sens   To have good way
To be sensible

SIÈGE   *SEAT*
Faire le siège   To make the seat
To lay siege to

Etat de siège   State of seat
Siege

Siège social   Social seat
Registered office

SIFFLET   *WHISTLE*

Il m'a coupé le sifflet   He cut me the whistle

He interrupted me

SITUATION   *JOB*

Résumer la situation   To resume the job

To sum up

SŒUR   *SISTER*

Et ta sœur ?   And about your sister ?

Mind your own business

SONNER   *TO RING*

Etre sonné   To be rung

To be knocked out

SORTIE   *WAY OUT*

Faire une sortie à   To make a way out to
quelqu'un   somebody

To bawl somebody out

SOUCI   *WORRY*

C'est le cadet de mes   It is the junior of my
soucis   worries

It is the last of my problems

SOURIS *MOUSE*
Une chauve-souris A bald mouse
A bat

SUISSE *SWISS*
Un petit-suisse A little Swiss
A soft cream cheese

Révision
R-S

I passed him a soap and I made a way
out to him because as he was round like
a tail of shovel he got a turn of kidneys
in carrying a heavy diet of bananas.

Je lui ai passé un savon et je lui ai fait
une sortie car comme il était rond
comme une queue de pelle, il a attrapé un
tour de reins en portant un lourd régime
de bananes.

Dix-huitième leçon
T-U

TABAC *TOBACCO*

C'est du même tabac It is of the same tobacco

It is the same

TABLEAU *PAINTING*

Brosser un tableau To brush a painting

To describe

Jouer sur les deux To play on the two
tableaux paintings

To lay odds both ways

TÂCHE *SPOT*

Se tuer à la tâche To kill oneself at the spot

To kill oneself working

TAPER   *TO HIT*
Se taper la cloche   To hit one's bell
To eat well

TAPISSERIE   *TAPESTRY*
Faire tapisserie   To make tapestry
To be a wallflower

TARTE   *PIE*
Ce n'est pas de la tarte !   It is not pie !
It is not easy!

TARTINE   *TOAST*
Ecrire des tartines   To write toasts
To write a lot

TEMPS   *TIME*
Un temps de chien   A time of dog
Bad weather

TENIR   *TO HOLD*
Un tiens vaut mieux   A hold is better than
que deux tu l'auras   two you will hold it
A bird in the hand is worth two in the bush

TÊTE   *HEAD*
Faire une sale tête   To make a dirty head
To have a nasty mug

Etre la tête de Turc   To be the turkish head
To be the scapegoat

Tête à queue   Head to tail
Slew

Tête-bêche   Head-spade
Top to bottom

TIMBRER   *TO STAMP*
Etre timbré   To be stamped
To be round the bend

TIRER   *TO SHOOT*
A tire-d'aile   At shoot-wing
Swiftly

TOMBER   *TO FALL*
Il tombe à point nommé   He falls at named point
He comes just in time

TOUR   *TOWER*
A double tour   At double tower
To double lock

Le Tour de France   The Tower of France
The round France cycle race

Faire un tour de cochon   To make a tower of pig
To trick

En un tour de main   On one tower of hand
In a flash

Le tour est joué   The tower is played
The trick has worked

TOURNER   *TO TURN*
Etre mal tourné   To be badly turned
To be in a bad mood

TOUT   *ALL*
Touche-à-tout   Touch-to-all
To have a finger in every pie

Jouer le tout pour le tout   To play the all for the all
To risk everything

Le Tout-Paris   The all-Paris
The smart set

TRADUIRE   *TO TRANSLATE*
Traduire quelqu'un   To translate somebody
en justice   in Court
To prosecute

TRAIN   *TRAIN*
Se magner le train   To move one's train
To hurry up

93

Filer le train   To spin the train
To follow

TRANQUILLE   *QUIET*
Tranquille comme   Quiet like Baptiste
Baptiste
Very quiet

TRAVAILLER   *TO WORK*
Travailler du chapeau   To work from the hat
To be crazy

TRENTE ET UN   *THIRTY ONE*
Se mettre sur son   To put oneself on one's
trente et un   thirty one
To dress up

TYPE   *GUY*
Avoir un type accentué   To have an accentued guy
To be marked

UN   *ONE*
Il était moins une   It was less one
It was a narrow escape

Cinq colonnes à la une   Five columns at the one
Front page

Dix-neuvième leçon
V

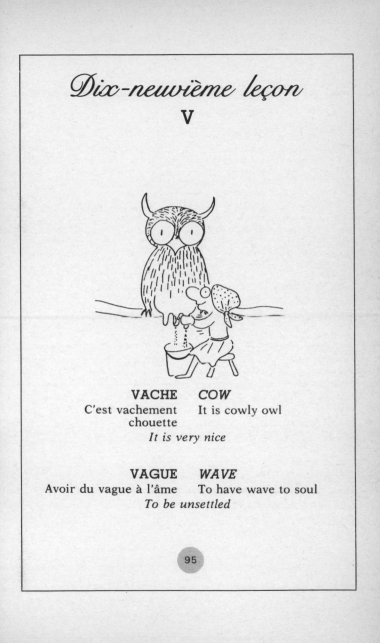

VACHE   *COW*
C'est vachement   It is cowly owl
chouette
It is very nice

VAGUE   *WAVE*
Avoir du vague à l'âme   To have wave to soul
To be unsettled

VALISE   *SUITCASE*

Se faire la valise   To make oneself the
suitcase

To leave

VASE   *MUD*

Etre vaseux   To be muddy

To be washed out

VEINE   *VEIN*

Avoir une veine de   To have a vein of
pendu   hanged

To be very lucky

VER   *WORM*

Ne pas être piqué des   Not to be picked by the
vers   worms

To be first rate

VERNIS   *VARNISH*

Etre verni   To be varnished

To be lucky

VERT   *GREEN*

Raconter des vertes et   To tell green and not
des pas mûres   ripe

To tell spicy

VESTE   *JACKET*

Ramasser une veste   To pick up a jacket
To fail

VIE   *LIFE*

Une vie de bâton de   A life of stick of chair
chaise
A rollicking life

VIEUX   *OLD*

Un vieux de la vieille   An old of the old
A very old person

VITE   *QUICK*

Vite fait sur le gaz   Quick made on the gas
Very fast

VIVRE   *TO LIVE*

Etre sur le qui-vive   To be on the who-lives
To be on the alert

VOIR   *TO SEE*

Un m'as-tu vu   A have you seen me
A conceited person

VOITURE   *CAR*

En voiture Simone !   In the car Simone !
Go ahead !

VOIX   *VOICE*

Avoir voix au chapitre   To have voice to the chapter

To have a say in the matter

VOL   *ROBERRY*

Faire du voi à voile   To do sailing robbery

To glide

VOULOIR   *TO WANT*

En veux-tu, en voilà   Do you want some, here there are

As many as you want

VUE   *SIGHT*

A vue de nez   At sight of nose

At a rough estimate

Vingtième leçon
W-X-Y-Z

WAGON *WAGON*
Un wagon-lit A bed-wagon
A sleeping car

X *X*
Il a fait l'X He made the X
He studied at the Polytechnic Institute

ZÈBRE *ZEBRA*
Un drôle de zèbre A funny zebra
A peculiar person

ZÉRO *ZERO*
Les avoir à zéro To have them at zero
To be frightened

ZOUAVE *MAN OF THE ALMA BRIDGE*

Faire le zouave   To make the man of
                   the Alma bridge

To brag

Révision
T à Z

I am badly turned because I made a head to tail during the Tower of France and I have them at zero because I am going to pick up a jacket.

Je suis mal tourné car j'ai fait un tête à queue pendant le Tour de France et je les ai à zéro parce que je vais ramasser une veste.

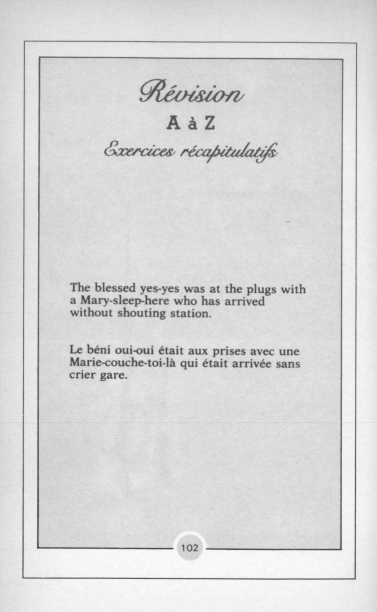

Révision

A à Z

Exercices récapitulatifs

The blessed yes-yes was at the plugs with
a Mary-sleep-here who has arrived
without shouting station.

Le béni oui-oui était aux prises avec une
Marie-couche-toi-là qui était arrivée sans
crier gare.

While their husbands were making the men of the Alma bridge with their scratched completes, the ladies were pancaking their buns.

Pendant que leurs maris faisaient les zouaves avec leurs complets rayés, les femmes se crépaient le chignon.

He brought back a strawberry, half-fig half-grape, after having lost the first sleeve.

Il ramena sa fraise, mi-figue mi-raisin, après avoir perdu la première manche.

He took back the hair from the beast in breaking the crust with a pot at the fire which cost him the eyes of the head.

Il a repris du poil de la bête en cassant la croûte d'un pot-au-feu qui lui avait coûté les yeux de la tête.

He had a tooth opposite her because she
put down a rabbit to him.

Il a une dent contre elle parce qu'elle lui
a posé un lapin.

Name of a pipe! It is not pie to make the
nice when one has fifty brooms.

Nom d'une pipe! Ce n'est pas de la tarte
de faire le beau quand on a cinquante
balais.

The bite-gentleman was not bathing in the oil, so he asked for a little Swiss.

Le croque-monsieur ne baignait pas dans l'huile, alors il a demandé un petit-suisse.

She was cowly owl and he was drawn at four pins but had films, so she refused to pass at the pan.

Elle était vachement chouette et il était tiré à quatre épingles mais avait des pellicules, alors elle refusa de passer à la casserole.

BRODARD ET TAUPIN À LA FLÈCHE (5-88)
DÉPÔT LÉGAL : FÉVRIER 1987. Nº 9485-4 (6511-5)

Collection Points

SÉRIE ACTUELS

Collection Points

SÉRIE ROMAN

Collection Points

SÉRIE POINT-VIRGULE

Collection Points

DERNIERS TITRES PARUS